CW01052191

CONT

Pedigree®

Published by Pedigree Books Limited
Beech Hill House, Walnut Gardens, Exeter, Devon EX4 4DH. Published 2009.

ASH

Ash Ketchum has a dream – to be the greatest Pokémon Master in the world. He's well on the way to achieving this goal. From humble beginnings in Pallet Town he's progressed through the regions of Kanto, Johto, Hoenn and Sinnoh, battling gym leaders, capturing Pokémon and increasing in knowledge and skill.

Ash is not without flaws – he's impetuous and sometimes overconfident, but his courage and determination inspire friendship and loyalty among the humans and Pokémon he meets. In fact many of Pokémon don't even wait to be caught by Ash during battle, choosing to follow him willingly instead. Now in the mountainous Sinnoh region, with his close friends by his side, Ash is ready to accept any challenge. Go Ash!

As the first of Ash's Pokémon, Pikachu holds a special place in the boy's heart. It is hard to believe that the pair got off to such a rocky start! Pikachu was only paired with Ash because he arrived late to meet Professor Oak and start his journey. All the other Pokémon had been taken, leaving Pikachu as the only option. The feisty Pokémon even refused to be transported in the Poké Ball, preferring to travel on Ash's shoulder.

The unlikely duo's rock-solid friendship was cemented when Ash saved Pikachu from an attack by a flock of wild Spearow, putting his own life at risk in the process. Who knows what excitements and perils await them now in Sinnoh? Whatever comes their way, the friends will face it together.

PIKACHU

BROCK

Every budding Pokémon trainer needs a cool friend like Brock. The former Gym Leader turned Breeder has an encyclopaedic knowledge of Pokémon which he's more than happy to share with his buddies. Brock and Ash met in Pewter City Gym where Brock was working, whilst dreaming of greater things. He'd always wanted to become a Breeder but in his father's absence was caring for his brothers and sisters. Luckily, Brock's dad returned, leaving him free to accompany Ash and finally follow his dreams.

Brock can't help showing his own fatherly side – he's mature, wise and a great cook to boot. His only weakness is pretty girls. Much to the amusement of his friends he can't seem to stop help falling head over heels in love!

DAWN

Dawn is the new kid on the block, and a fantastic addition to the gang. She has just begun her journey but is positive, plucky and prefers to look to the future. Her goal is to become a great Pokémon Coordinator like her mother Johanna. This means entering her Pokémon in contests where they are judged on beauty rather than power.

Dawn has a great sense of style and loves to look her best – she originally set out on her journey with a huge suitcase full of dresses! Luckily her mum persuaded her to leave the frocks at home. Now she's on the road it's important that Dawn travels light so that she's always battle-ready.

Jessie, James and their sly, spiky, Pokémon Meowth, are the sworn enemies of Ash and his pals. Team Rocket have an evil plan to take over the world using Pokémon and they don't care what they have to do to make it happen!

The team's boss Giovanni has specifically requested that they steal Ash's unique Pikachu. The bumbling trio set out to hamper Ash at every turn and although so far – much to Giovanni's annoyance – all their attempts have failed, they continue to think up even more complex and crazy schemes. Team Rocket has no problem breaking rules or exploiting Pokémon for money. Luckily they seem to be no match for our heroes.

TEAM ROCKET

SHAYMIN

LAND FORME

TYPE:	GRASS
ABILITY:	NATURAL CURE
HEIGHT:	0.2m
WEIGHT:	2.1kg

SKY FORME

TYPE:	GRASS/FLYING
ABILITY:	SERENE GRACE
HEIGHT:	0.4m
WEIGHT:	5.2kg

Shaymin is one of the smallest known mysterious Pokémon ever sighted in the Sinnoh region. The timid hedgehog-like creature dwells in flower patches, camouflaging itself amongst the blooms. When exposed to Gracidea flowers, it turns into the more courageous Sky Forme, returning to its original land state when night falls. Shaymin uses the unique Seed Flare move to dissolve impurities in the air, replacing polluted areas with lush flower fields.

This pair of Pokémon are not believed to have any evolutions, but they are both able to morph into breathtaking new shapes!

GIRATINA

ORIGIN FORME

TYPE:	**GHOST/DRAGON**
ABILITY:	**LEVITATE**
HEIGHT:	**6.9m**
WEIGHT:	**650kg**

ALTERED FORME

TYPE:	**GHOST/DRAGON**
ABILITY:	**PRESSURE**
HEIGHT:	**4.5m**
WEIGHT:	**750kg**

It is said that Giratina lives in a reverse world on the flip side of our own reality. In this mirror realm, Pokémon professors believe that Giratina takes on its origin forme. In Sinnoh, the legendary creature shows itself in its altered centipede-like state. The Pokémon is capable of wielding great force and is able to mount Ghost, Dark, Psychic and Electrical attacks. If its home is under threat, Giratina will do anything to protect it.

BIBAREL

TYPE:	NORMAL-WATER
ABILITY:	SIMPLE-UNAWARE
HEIGHT:	1.0m
WEIGHT:	31.5kg

Evolved from Bidoof, it makes its nest by damming streams. Like many aquatic creatures it is sluggish on land, but once in water, Bibarel can swim like lightning.

PIPLUP

TYPE:	WATER
ABILITY:	TORRENT
HEIGHT:	0.4m
WEIGHT:	5.2kg

The penguin-like Pokémon favoured by Dawn, is a skilled swimmer and diver which dwells and hunts on the shores of the northern lakes. It evolves into Prinplup and Empoleon.

CROAGUNK

TYPE:	POISON-FIGHTING
ABILITY:	ANTICIPATION-DRY SKIN
HEIGHT:	0.7m
WEIGHT:	23.0kg

Its cheeks hold poison sacs which inflate, emitting an intimidating blubbering sound that helps it catch foes off guard. Croagunk evolves into the hideous Toxicroak.

MACHOKE

TYPE:	FIGHTING
ABILITY:	GUTS-NO GUARD
HEIGHT:	1.5m
WEIGHT:	70.5kg

Machoke's boundless power could be extremely dangerous, so it wears a belt that suppresses its energy. Both of its arms are swollen with muscle.

MACHAMP

TYPE:	FIGHTING
ABILITY:	GUTS-NO GUARD
HEIGHT:	1.6m
WEIGHT:	130kg

Having evolved from Machoke, this Pokémon punches with its four arms at blinding speeds. During battle, it can launch 1,000 punches in just two seconds.

BUIZEL

TYPE:	WATER
ABILITY:	SWIFT SWIM
HEIGHT:	0.7m
WEIGHT:	29.5kg

Buizel swims by rotating its two tails like a screw, boasting a collar-like flotation sac which inflates on water and collapses when it dives under the surface.

TURTWIG

TYPE:	GRASS
ABILITY:	OVERGROW
HEIGHT:	0.4m
WEIGHT:	10.2kg

Turtwig makes oxygen with its body by using photosynthesis. The leaf on its head wilts and its shell softens when it's thirsty. The grass Pokémon evolves to Grotle and then Torterra.

CHIMCHAR

TYPE:	FIRE
ABILITY:	BLAZE
HEIGHT:	0.5m
WEIGHT:	6.2kg

A great climber, it lives on mountain tops and evolves to Monferno then Infernape. Nothing can extinguish Chimchar's fire, although the flame goes out by itself when it sleeps.

SUDOWOODO

TYPE:	ROCK
ABILITY:	STURDY-ROCK HEAD
HEIGHT:	1.2m
WEIGHT:	38kg

Even more tree-like than it's first form Bonsly, Sudowoodo's body is actually closer to rocks and stones than wood. The Pokémon has a low resistance to water.

TEAM ROCKET'S TRAP

Oh no! Pikachu has fallen asleep in the forest and has been left behind. Help him find the right path to bring him safely back to Ash. But beware! Three of the four paths will lead him straight into a Team Rocket trap.

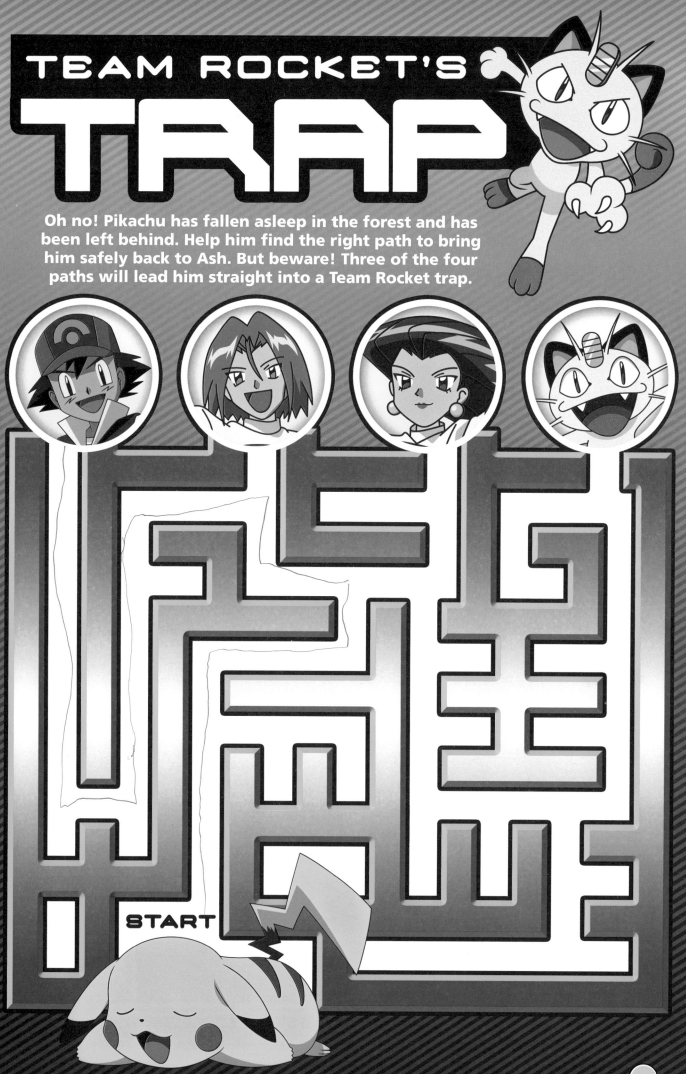

START

COOL COLOUR COPY

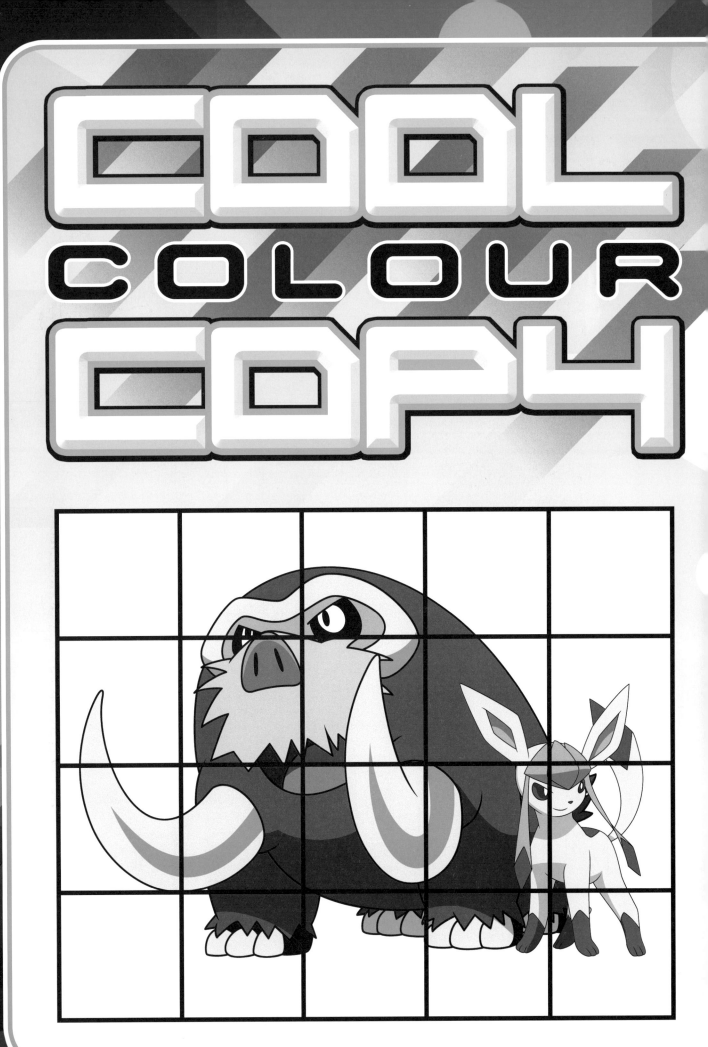

Check out these awesome new Sinnoh ice-types, Glaceon and Mamoswine. These über-cool customers are itching to be copied and coloured. Once you've drawn them into the grid, why not use felt-tips or pencils to give them a frosty feel!

BIBAREL GNAWS BEST!

AN UNFINISHED BRIDGE THREATENS TO KEEP OUR HEROES FROM REACHING SOLACEON TOWN IN TIME FOR DAWN'S NEXT POKÉMON CONTEST. WHO IS THE MYSTERIOUS AND LAZY STONE-CUTTER RESPONSIBLE FOR THE DELAY AND HAS BROCK FINALLY FOUND THE PERFECT GIRL?

Ash, Brock and Dawn stared in dismay at the cavernous gorge ahead and the half-finished bridge standing across it. They'd been walking for days now, but it seemed that their journey was destined to take even longer.
"It looks like we're not getting across the river that way," sighed Ash. "There's someone up there."
Brock's eyes widened as he homed in on the group standing on the precarious and unstable structure. It seemed like a pretty girl was being inched towards the edge by two mean-looking guys!
"I'll save you my lady," he yelled, bounding off before the others could stop him.

On the bridge the girl and men were deep in conversation.

"So what are you going to do about this?" said a stocky guy in a hard hat. "You know there's no time left."

Brock's shouts interrupted him. "Don't Moooove!!"

The group turned and stepped aside just in time to see the Pokémon Breeder hurtle between them and plummet over the edge. Brock's body seemed to fall backwards in slow motion. Was this be the end for him? Suddenly, from nowhere, a blue toad-like arm reached out and grabbed hold of Brock's flailing hand.

"I owe you, Croagunk," gasped Brock, as the faithful Pokémon heaved him back to safety. "You kids should know better than to hang around here," scolded the man, as Ash and Dawn arrived panting at the bridge.

"I'm here to save this beautiful lady!" replied Brock angrily.

"You're making a mistake," said the girl, introducing herself as Isis. "The head engineer and I were discussing the construction of the bridge."

"Look's like lover boy's done it again," giggled Dawn.

"This bridge will be completed in three days' time even if those Pokémon collapse from exhaustion," stormed the engineer, walking away with the Mayor.

Isis's face fell. She explained that she'd been hired to oversee the stonecutting after the master stone cutter had injured his back, but that work had ground to a halt.

"Leave it to me," said Brock, preparing some bowls of his special Pokémon food. The Machamp and Machoke workers devoured it immediately.

"That's great," said Isis, "except they aren't the real problem."

Lurking behind some bushes, Jessie, James and Meowth were eavesdropping as usual.
"A group of Pokémon with the bulk to build bridges has the brawn to build us a base!" gasped James to Jessie.
"And after they're through with our project, we could hand them to the Boss!" added Meowth.
"Building a glorious future…" said Jessie.
"…one Sinnoh stone at a time," smirked James.

Isis led Brock and the confused group away into to a deserted quarry. She sadly pointed upwards to a hole in the rock from where snoring could be heard.
"Our stones are cut by the Pokémon up on that ledge." Ash pointed his Pokédex in the direction of the snores.

BIBAREL
THE BEAVER POKÉMON. IT DAMS UP RIVERS TO MAKE ITS NEST AND IS WELL KNOWN AS AN INDUSTRIOUS WORKER.

"Doesn't look like an industrious worker to me," said Dawn.
"A good napper though," added Ash.
Before Isis could reply, Brock was whipping up another batch of his famous food.
"Just one bowl and you'll be itching to cut stone!" he said, attaching the basin to a pole and hoisting it up towards Bibarel.

The instant it smelled the food, Bibarel woke up and gobbled the lot.
"What did I tell you?" laughed Brock.
But Bibarel simply turned over and went back to sleep, sending the bowl crashing down onto Brock's head.
"What's up with that?!" he cried.
"Are you sure Bibarel's a first class stone cutter?" Ash asked.
"I'm the one who taught Bibarel to cut stone at the Pokémon Training Centre," Isis admitted shyly.
Brock couldn't believe his ears. "Are you a professional Pokémon Breeder?"
"Yes, but I'm not proud of it," she whispered. "I can't even motivate my workers."
Isis told the gang how she'd coached Bibarel before sending him to a master stone-cutter to perfect his art. "Bibarel never took a day off until its teacher stopped coming to visit."
"So Bibarel's missing its teacher!" exclaimed Brock.

Brock told Isis not to worry, then asked Ash to borrow Turtwig, Buizel and Chimchar. "Quick Sudowoodo, you too!" he added.
Piplup also wanted in on the action.
Brock's orders came thick and fast. "Chimchar heat the stone with Flamethrower. Now Buizel, cool it down using Water Gun!"
The stone cracked.

"Turtwig use Razor Leaf. Sudowoodo Use Razor Leaf with Mimic!"
In a few seconds a pile of neatly hewn stones stood before them.
"I'm afraid this is no good," said Isis.
"The blocks have to be exactly the right dimensions."
Suddenly Bibarel woke up.

"I don't like that look on Bibarel's face," said Dawn.
Before the others could agree or Bibarel could strike, there was a commotion from the camp.
"It sounds like the Machamp and Machoke!" cried Brock.
"Oh no!" shouted Isis. "Look up there!"
A hot air balloon emblazoned with the telltale letter R hung in the sky. Below it swung a cage full of Isis's construction crew. Captured!
"Listen up," rang the familiar voices of Team Rocket. "The movers and shakers are here, broadcasting live, loud and clear!"
Suddenly a mechanical arm reached down from the balloon, grabbed Bibarel and threw him into the cage with the rest of the workers.

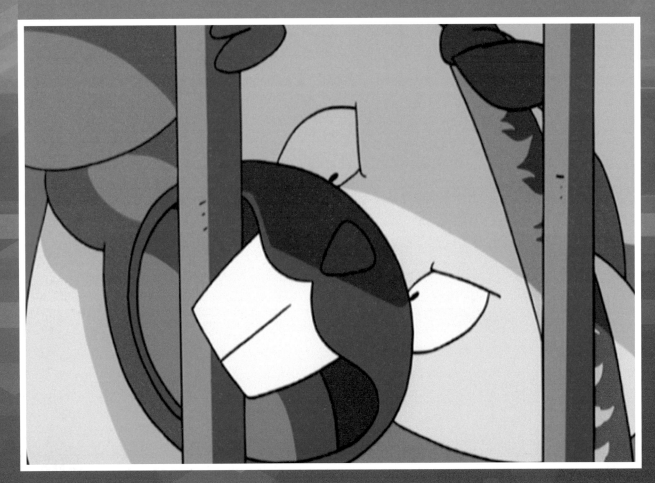

Quick as lightning, Ash called up Chimchar, Buizel and Turtwig.
"Use Razor Leaf," he commanded as Brock instructed Sudowoodo to do the same. Nothing worked.
"Now what do we do?" cried Ash in despair.
Luckily the worried gang had forgotten Bibarel's greatest weapon – its teeth!

"Uh-oh," gulped James. "It's gnawing the bars!"
Down on the ground Ash smiled at Pikachu. "I think this'd be a great time to use Thunderbolt."
There was a huge explosion as Pikachu's power destroyed the balloon. Team Rocket fell to the ground still bickering about where things went wrong. It was time to blast off.

"You were wonderful Bibarel," praised Isis. "You saved them all!"

"How about you doing a little stonecutting now?' pleaded Brock.

Everyone sighed as the stubborn Bibarel just turned away.

There was a crunch of tracks on gravel and the furious engineer stepped down from his digger.

"You can't be trusted to get the job done, can you?" he yelled. The engineer pulled a Poké Ball from his jacket and summoned Rhydon. "Use your horn drill to cut that stone!"

Isis tried to explain that without Bibarel's help the stone would not be correctly cut, but the engineer just urged Rhydon on. It was the prompt Bibarel needed. Suddenly it leapt at Rhydon, mauling him to the ground.

"I guess you wanna fight," said the engineer, bringing out Aggron, Magmar and Metang. "Aggron, use Iron Head! Metang, Metal Claw! Magmar use Flamethrower!"

Bibarel did his best to avoid the blows, but he was hopelessly outnumbered.

"Time to even up the sides," said Ash. "Pikachu! Iron Tail, let's go!"

As Pikachu battled Aggron, the gang called Chimchar, Buizel, Turtwig, Sudowoodo and even Piplup to join him. Their combined force sent the engineer's Pokémon crashing to the floor in a heap.

But even without his Pokémon, the engineer was not going to give in.
"All right you punks," he seethed, climbing up to the controls of his digger. "I'm gonna finish that bridge if it's the last thing I do!'
As the machine surged forward, a huge boulder knocked it sideways.
"Who did that?" screamed the engineer, climbing from the wreckage.
"I did," called a voice. The gang looked up to see the master stone-cutter riding on the shoulder of a Machamp.
"Does this mean your back is healed?' asked Isis excitedly.
"The truth is I never hurt it," replied the stone-cutter. "This blueprint was the only thing that needed to be healed."
The man explained that the engineer's blueprint was flawed and that, had the bridge been constructed to his plan, it would have collapsed.

"Why did you do this?" raged Isis.
"Because we never would have finished it in time and my reputation would be ruined," replied the engineer.
"Get off this site!" screamed the stone-cutter. Bibarel, the Machamp and Machoke together with Ash and Brock's Pokémon squared up to the disgraced engineer, who turned on his heel and ran.
"Without a blueprint we'll never get done in

time," gasped Isis.
The stone-cutter revealed that he had already made a new one. The crew immediately set to work headed by an excited Bibarel. Chimchar, Buizel, Croagunk and the gang dug out the stone, Piplup and Pikachu carried blocks to the bridge and Machamp and Machoke laid them. It was hard work, but together they finished it. Just in time.

As the fireworks of the opening ceremony lit up the sky, Ash, Brock, Dawn, Isis and the master stone-cutter admired the finished bridge.

"You've done a wonderful job, Isis!" said the stone-cutter.

"I certainly had a lot of help sir," she admitted sheepishly. "It's embarrassing for a Pokémon Breeder to not know how Bibarel was feeling."

"If you work together with your Pokémon the way you just did, I guarantee you'll make an excellent Pokémon Breeder," he smiled. The stone-cutter turned to Ash, Brock and Dawn and handed them each an embroidered bandana.

"This will look great when I'm competing in my next contest," said the ever stylish Dawn. "Thank you!"

It was time for the trio to leave, but as usual Brock couldn't let his feelings go unheard. "I was wondering if you would build us a bridge of love connecting our hearts forever?' he asked Isis passionately, before letting out a scream and collapsing to the floor. Croagunk, eager to stop Brock from making a fool of himself again, had jabbed him with its toxic fingers!

So our heroes are once again on the road to Solaceon Town, with the added satisfaction of having helped a new friend in need.

PART 1

POKÉMON TRAINER TEST

So you want to be a Pokémon Trainer? Take this tricky three-part test to see if you truly have what it takes. You'll need to draw on all your knowledge. Check your answers with those in the back of the book, and when you're ready, move on to the next level.

1. What type of Pokémon is Pikachu?

A :: Normal	☐
B :: Electric	☑
C :: Ground	☐

2. Which Pokémon is this? 》》》》》》》

A :: Croagunk	☑
B :: Toxicroak	☐
C :: Chingling	☐

3. What does Turtwig have growing out of his head?

A :: A twig	☑
B :: Horns	☐
C :: Another head	☐

4. What type of Pokémon is Sudowoodo?

A :: Rock	☑
B :: Wood	☐
C :: Normal	☐

5. Machamp is an evolution of which Pokémon?

A :: Mime Jr ☐
B :: Mesprit ☐
C :: Machoke ☑

6. Which Pokémon is this?

A :: Lopunny ☐
B :: Buneary ☑
C :: Budew ☐

7. What type of Pokémon is Luxio?

A :: Electric ☑
B :: Water ☐
C :: Rock ☐

8. Which of these Pokémon is Dawn's special friend?

A :: Pikachu ☐
B :: Piplup ☑
C :: Psyduck ☐

9. Which Pokémon is this?

A :: Infernape ☐
B :: Monferno ☐
C :: Chimchar ☑

10. What type of Pokémon is Bibarel?

A :: Water-Rock ☐
B :: Rock-Fighting ☐
C :: Normal-Water ☑

The test continues on page 32!

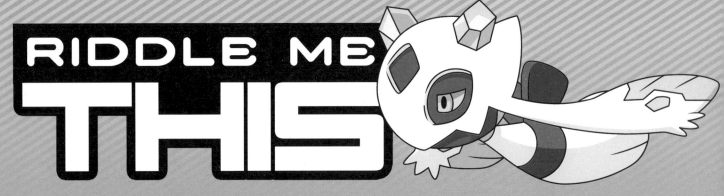

RIDDLE ME THIS

Can you work out which Pokémon is described in this riddle? Each line is a clue, revealing one letter of its name. When you've worked out the clues, write the letters in the boxes, and then read downwards to uncover the identity of this fiery Pokémon.

My first is in Bibarel, but not in Brock, ☐

My second lies in Cranidos, tough as a rock, ☐

My third starts the thing which burns at Chimchar's rear, ☐

My fourth has a beak and claws, it would appear, ☐

My fifth starts the name of a devious team, ☐

This Pokémon's eyes catch the tiniest gleam. ☐

My seventh is Ketchum, the hero du jour, ☐

My eighth, his best friend, you know him I'm sure, ☐

My ninth starts a word meaning 'change' is a-foot... ☐

I am Chimchar's third stage; now let's see what you put!

....

26

FROM

TO

'From me to you' says Pikachu!

MAKE YOUR OWN
POKÉMON POP-UP CARD

A perky smile from Pikachu would make anyone's day – so why not send a hello to someone in your Pokémon posse. You could also use this cool pop-up card to cheer up a friend or save it for someone's birthday.

YOU WILL NEED: PVA GLUE & A PEN

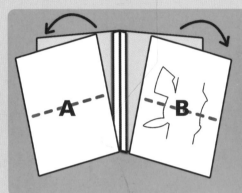

STEP 1
Tear out card pieces A and B from this book, following the perforated edges. These will make the inner and outer sections of your greetings card.

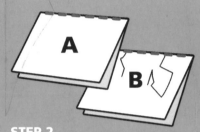

STEP 2
Fold both pieces in half along the dotted lines.

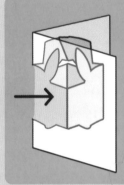

STEP 3
Push out the Pikachu-shaped pop up and, press it through towards the centre of the card. Fold along the dotted lines on either side of Pikachu, in the opposite direction to the main crease.

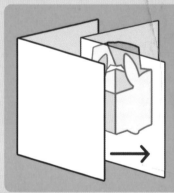

STEP 4
Apply glue around the inside edges of piece A. Slot piece B inside A and stick down firmly. Allow the glue to dry.

STEP 5 Now write your message inside!

YANMEGA

TYPE:	BUG-FLYING
ABILITY:	SPEED BOOST-TINTED LENS
HEIGHT:	1.9m
WEIGHT:	51.5kg

Evolved from Yanma, Yanmega churns its wings, creating shock waves capable of inflicting critical internal injuries to its foes.

LEAFEON

TYPE:	GRASS
ABILITY:	LEAF GUARD
HEIGHT:	1.0m
WEIGHT:	25.5kg

Leafon is one of Eevee's seven evolutions. Just like a plant, the Pokémon uses photosynthesis. As a result, it is always enveloped in clear air.

GLACEON

TYPE:	ICE
ABILITY:	SNOW CLOAK
HEIGHT:	0.8m
WEIGHT:	25.9kg

As a protective technique, it can completely freeze its fur to make its hairs stand up like needles. Glaceon is another of Eevee's seven evolutions.

GLISCOR

TYPE:	GROUND-FLYING
ABILITY:	HYPER CUTTER-SAND VEIL
HEIGHT:	2.0m
WEIGHT:	42.5kg

Gliscor observes prey while hanging upside down from branches. When the chance presents itself, it swoops! The Pokémon evolves from the ferocious Gligar.

MAMOSWINE

TYPE:	ICE-GROUND
ABILITY:	OBLIVIOUS-SNOW CLOAK
HEIGHT:	2.5m
WEIGHT:	291.0kg

It evolves from Swinub and Piloswine into an impressive beast with blue markings around the eyes, and tusks of ice. Its species declined after the passing of the ice age.

PORYGON-Z

TYPE:	NORMAL
ABILITY:	ADAPTABILITY-DOWNLOAD
HEIGHT:	0.9m
WEIGHT:	34.0kg

This programmed Pokémon evolved from Porygon and Porygon-2. Additional software was installed to make it a better Pokémon in its third evolution. It still began acting oddly however.

GALLADE

TYPE:	PYSCHIC-FIGHTING
ABILITY:	STEADFAST
HEIGHT:	1.6m
WEIGHT:	52.0kg

A master of courtesy and swordsmanship, it fights using extending swords on its elbows. Along with Gardevoir, Gallade originated from Ralts and Kirlia.

PROBOPAS

TYPE:	ROCK-STEEL
ABILITY:	STURDY-MAGNET PULL
HEIGHT:	1.4m
WEIGHT:	340.0kg

Evolved from Nosepass, this Pokémon is strongly magnetic. It also controls three small independent units called Mini-Noses.

DUSKNOIR

TYPE:	GHOST
ABILITY:	PRESSURE
HEIGHT:	2.2m
WEIGHT:	106.6kg

This spooky Pokémon has antenna which capture radio waves from the world of spirits that command it to take people there. It evolved from Duskull and Dusclops.

FROSLASS

TYPE:	ICE-GHOST
ABILITY:	SNOW CLOAK
HEIGHT:	1.3m
WEIGHT:	26.6kg

It freezes foes using its chill-ridden breath, blasting frosts of over -50°C. The area that seems to be its body is actually hollow. Froslass evolved with Glalie from Snorunt.

ROTOM

TYPE:	ELECTRIC-GHOST
ABILITY:	LEVITATE
HEIGHT:	0.3m
WEIGHT:	0.3kg

Rotom's body is composed of plasma. It should be kept away from electronic devices as it is known to infiltrate them and wreak havoc. Rotom has no evolutions.

CRESSELIA

TYPE:	PSYCHIC
ABILITY:	LEVITATE
HEIGHT:	1.5m
WEIGHT:	85.6kg

Shiny particles are released from Cresselia's wings like a gauzy veil. This Pyschic Pokémon is said to represent the crescent moon.

PHIONE

TYPE:	WATER
ABILITY:	HYDRATION
HEIGHT:	0.4m
WEIGHT:	3.1kg

This Pokémon thrives in warm seas. It uses the flotation sac on its head to drift for miles as it searches for areas rich in food.

CRANIDOS

TYPE:	ROCK
ABILITY:	MOLD BREAKER
HEIGHT:	0.9m
WEIGHT:	31.5kg

Cranidos roamed in jungles around 100 million years ago. With an awesomely tough skull, the Rock Pokémon morphs into the still tougher Rampardos.

NOCTOWL

TYPE:	NORMAL-FLYING
ABILITY:	INSOMNIA-KEEN EYE
HEIGHT:	1.6m
WEIGHT:	40.8kg

Noctowl evolves from Hootowl. The bird Pokémon has amazing vision, enabling it to pick out the shapes of faraway objects using just the tiniest glimmer of light.

PART 2

POKÉMON TRAINER TEST

Well done, you've made it to Round Two! You're one step closer to graduating as a bonafide trainer. From here on the questions get a little bit tougher, so dig deep!

11. What is the most noticeable difference between Machoke and Machamp?

A :: Machoke has two more arms than Machamp ☐
B :: Machamp has two more arms than Machoke ☑
C :: Machoke has a crest on his head,
Machamp does not ☐

12. What is the name of this Pokémon?

A :: Froslass ☐
B :: Leafeon ☐
C :: Glaceon ☑

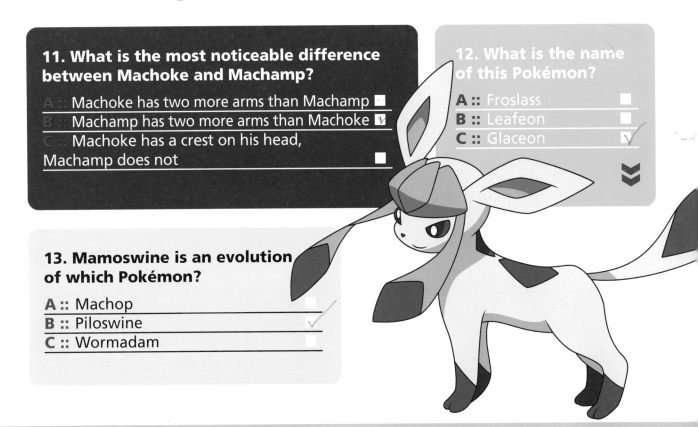

13. Mamoswine is an evolution of which Pokémon?

A :: Machop ☐
B :: Piloswine ☑
C :: Wormadam ☐

14. What type of Pokémon is Gallade?

A :: Ground-Fighting ☐
B :: Physic-Fighting ☑
C :: Ghost-Fighting ☐

15. How many legs does Yanmega have?

A :: Four ☐
B :: Eight ☐
C :: Six ☑

16. What is the name of this Pokémon?

A :: Porygon-Z ☑
B :: Porygon-2 ☐
C :: Porygon ☐

17. Where does Phione prefer to live?

A :: Desert plains ☐
B :: Warm seas ☑
C :: Remote caves ☐

18. Which of the following is not true of Pikachu?

A :: It stores electricity in its cheek pouches ☐
B :: It throws thunderbolts from its tail ☐
C :: It changes colour during gym battles. ☑

19. Noctowl's main power is:

A :: Keen eyes ☑
B :: Sharp claws ☐
C :: Lethal beak ☐

20. Only one of these Pokémon has evolved from others. Which is it?

A :: Probopass ☑
B :: Rotom ☐
C :: Cresselia ☐

The test continues on page 36!

BREAK BROCK'S CODE

With Team Rocket always on the prowl, our heroes have to be extra cautious about what they say. Someone has sent a letter to Isis, the stone-cutter in the story. Can you help her read it? Each of the five Pokémon correspond to a vowel. Match them up to crack the code.

A	B	I	O	U

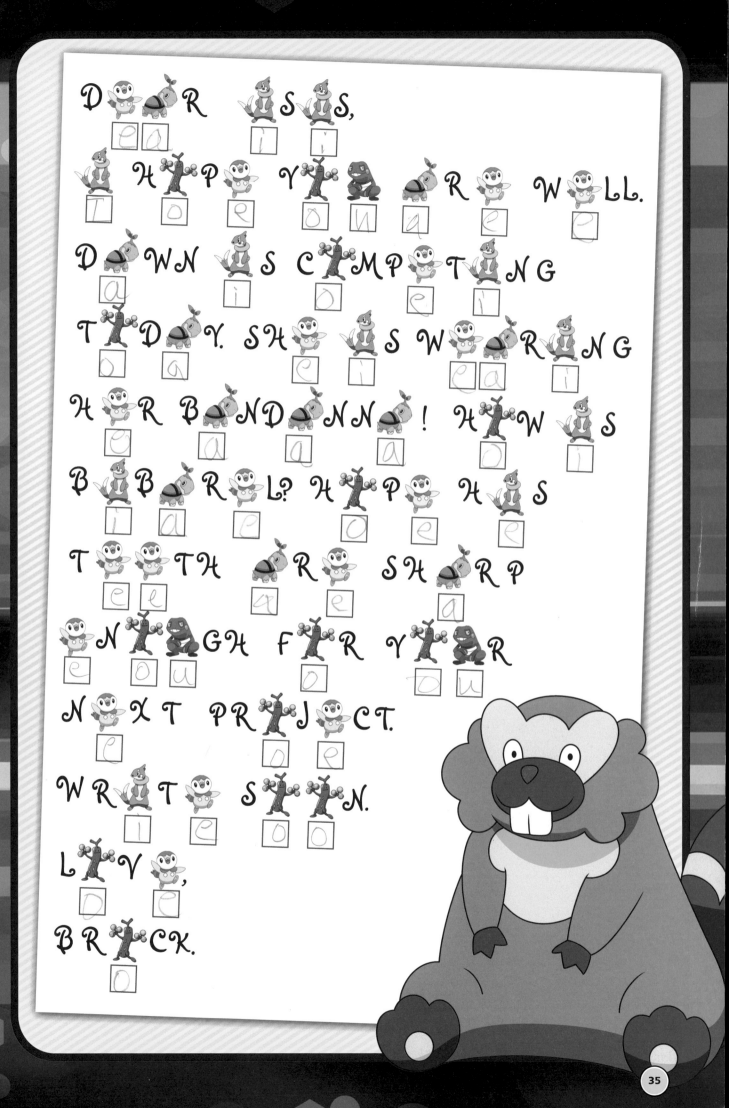

PART 3

POKÉMON
TRAINER TEST

Well done! You've reached the final stage. You're playing with the big boys now, but do you know enough to graduate as a fully-fledged trainer? Once you have finished the test, add up your scores from the previous rounds and see how you've done.

21. The birth of which legendary Sinnoh Pokémon is said to have started the movement of time itself?

A :: Palkia ☐
B :: Dialga ☑
C :: Azelf ☐

22. Which of these Pokémon is the heaviest?

A :: Yanmega ☐
B :: Gliscor ☐
C :: Gallade ☑

23. What is the name of Team Rocket's mysterious boss?

A :: Giovanni ☑
B :: Gianluco ☐
C :: Giancarlos ☐

24. What colour are the tips of Leafeon's ears and tail?

A :: Brown ☐
B :: Blue ☐
C :: Green ☑

25. How many different Pokémon evolve from Eevee?

A :: Six ☐
B :: Seven ☑
C :: Eight ☐

26. What does Shieldon evolve into?

A :: Bastiodon ☑
B :: Rhydon ☐
C :: Aggron ☐

27. What can Buizel do with its two tails to help it swim?

A :: Rotate them fast ☐
B :: Flap them like fins ☑
C :: Inflate them for buoyancy ☐

28. How many years had one Bronzong famously been sleeping when it was dug up on a construction site?

A :: 200 years ☐
B :: 2,000 years ☑
C :: 20,000 years ☐

29. Which of these Pokémon is the smallest?

A :: Chimchar ☐
B :: Bibarel ☐
C :: Rotom ☑

30. What type of Pokémon is Stunky?

A :: Poison-dark ☑
B :: Grass-poison ☐
C :: Grass-dark ☐

IF YOU SCORED BETWEEN 1 – 10
YOU ARE A NOVICE

You'll find it hard to train Pokémon while you've still so much to learn yourself. You'll need to study harder and clock up many more battles before you can truly call yourself a Trainer. Keep going, you can do it!

IF YOU SCORED BETWEEN 11 - 20
YOU ARE INTERMEDIATE

Well done. You're well on your way to achieving your goal. Continue on your journey and maybe find yourself a Pokémon clan like Ash's crew to swap info and tips with and make it all the more fun.

IF YOU SCORED BETWEEN 21 – 30
YOU ARE A PRO

Congratulations! You're a professional Pokémon Trainer. Your knowledge and skill are second to none! The world of Pokémon is ever-changing however, so you'll need to keep learning to stay on top.

Turn to page 38 to make yourself a cut out and keep certificate for your wall.

CUT OUT AND KEEP
CERTIFICATE

Why not fill in this wicked certificate to show the world just how much you've learnt about the world of Pokémon. Take the quiz first, to find your level.

Certificate of Pokémon Competence

POKéMON
DIAMOND AND PEARL

This is to certify that

_____

has successfully completed the Diamond & Pearl Trainer Test Parts 1 – 3 and is now a fully-fledged and highly skilled Pokémon Trainer

Level attained:

Pro

_____

Date: Spring 2009

WATERY WORDSEARCH

Can you spot Sinnoh's water-types lurking in this watery word puzzle? Check them off from the list below.

A	F	C	M	S	O	E	E	D	D	O	O	N	V	A	L	M
Q	A	H	A	A	E	P	I	Z	S	L	E	Z	I	U	B	K
U	C	B	A	R	A	A	E	K	O	W	N	S	G	E	Q	T
A	W	U	P	E	J	N	I	P	G	O	O	G	T	W	U	A
F	P	R	L	P	O	G	O	L	D	E	E	N	P	A	I	C
R	H	G	O	N	Q	B	E	O	N	E	H	E	H	S	A	R
E	I	N	J	Z	B	M	A	O	L	A	G	U	S	H	R	U
W	O	I	X	O	K	A	E	C	L	O	V	X	U	I	U	E
J	N	U	O	L	O	N	R	A	G	P	A	G	M	E	D	L
E	E	Y	S	A	I	T	I	T	R	J	I	P	M	E	O	V
O	U	R	S	M	E	Y	O	N	I	I	H	P	T	A	U	F
U	P	E	U	P	J	K	E	E	G	J	A	S	L	U	S	I
O	I	L	V	H	T	E	N	T	R	O	V	A	F	U	A	S
M	E	L	M	O	I	R	A	N	I	M	T	G	A	G	P	A
F	B	I	L	E	A	O	R	H	U	S	L	K	N	A	E	B
X	A	T	I	H	A	S	P	P	S	Y	D	U	C	K	E	E
C	F	C	N	E	T	F	W	D	I	E	S	I	R	O	N	E
U	A	O	J	O	P	I	K	A	F	A	G	L	O	U	T	F

Buizel ☐   **Goldeen** ☐   **Mantyke** ☐   **Phione** ☐   **Psyduck** ☐

Feebas ☐   **Lumineon** ☐   **Octillery** ☐   **Piplup** ☐   **Tentacool** ☐

PICK A PIKACHU

This page is charged up to the max with Pikachu! Can you find an identical pair hiding somewhere amongst these pictures? You'll need to drawn on all your powers of observation.

THE IDENTICAL PAIR ARE:

POKÉMON MIND PLAY

To be a formidable Pokémon master, you'll need to speed up your thought processes and learn to pre-empt your opponents' moves in battle. To prepare yourself, try training your mind with the following exercise:

1 :: Think of a number between 1 and 10.

2 :: Add 5.

3 :: Subtract 2.

4 :: Now subtract the number that you first thought of.

5 :: What is the number you're left with?

6 :: Flick to the answers page and you'll find it written there. Amazing!

Now why not play the game with your friends?

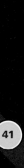

EYE EYE BOSS

Team Rocket boss Giovanni has ordered Jessie and James to swot up on their Pokémon. Meowth has taken photos of some new Pokémon they've come across, but as usual he's botched the job. Can you match and identify the extreme eye close-ups with the correct Pokémon below?

A

B

C

D

E

F

G

H

1.

2.

3.

4.

5.

6.

7.

8.

DASTARDLY DOT-TO-DOT

Evil Team Rocket never travel alone. Join the dots to see which Pokémon the terrible trio are hanging out with, then label them, picking names from the list below.

- CARNIVINE
- MIME JR
- DUSTOX
- WOBBUFFET
- SEVIPER

SHAPESHIFTER SHADOWS

1

GLIGAR →

2

→ MACHOKE →

3

SWINUB →

4

→ INFERNAPE

5

BIDOOF →

6

→ SKUNTANK

7

→ GROTLE →

8

→   →

Your studies of Pokémon will have taught you that most evolve into other forms during their lifetime. Study the dark shapes below and try to identify the missing evolutions of each Pokémon shown.

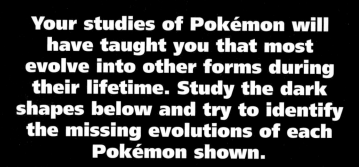

9

SNORUNT →

10

→

11

BONSLY →

12

→   → LUXRAY

13

→ LOPUNNY

14

PICHU →

HALL OF FAME
VS
WALL OF SHAME

Pokémon Hall of Fame

In the world of Pokémon there are the good guys and the really quite bad guys. They all want fame and glory but only some truly merit it.

Look at the list opposite and unravel the anagrams one-by-one to find the characters' names. Then add them to either the **Great Pokémon Hall of Fame** or the **Wall of Shame.** Can you draw their picture too? Look back through this book to remind yourself how they look.

- MAJES
- A HICK UP
- WE MOTH
- EEJISS
- WAND
- HAS
- BORCK

POKÉMON WALL OF SHAME

ANSWERS

Page 13
Team Rocket's Trap

Page 24
Pokémon Trainer Test – P1

1.**B**, 2.**A**, 3.**A**, 4.**A**, 5.**C**, 6.**B**, 7.**A**, 8.**B**, 9.**C**, 10.**C**.

Page 26
Riddle Me This

I is in Bibarel but not Brock.
N is in Cranidos.
F starts the word Fire – which Chimchar has instead of a tail.
E is the first letter of Empoleon from the picture clue.
R is the first letter of Rocket – the devious team.
N is the first letter of Noctowl from the picture clue.
A is first letter of Ash.
P stands for Pikachu, his best buddy.
E begins the word Evolution which means change for Pokémon.

INFERNAPE is the Chimchar's 3rd evolution.

Page 32
Pokémon Trainer Test – P2

11.**B**, 12.**C**, 13.**B**, 14.**B**, 15.**C**, 16.**A**, 17.**B**, 18.**C**, 19.**A**, 20.**A**.

Page 34
Break Brock's Code

Letter reads:
Dear Isis, I hope you are well. We are in Solaceon Town. Dawn is competing today. She is wearing her bandanna! How is Bibarel? Hope his teeth are sharp enough for your next project.
Write soon. Love, Brock.